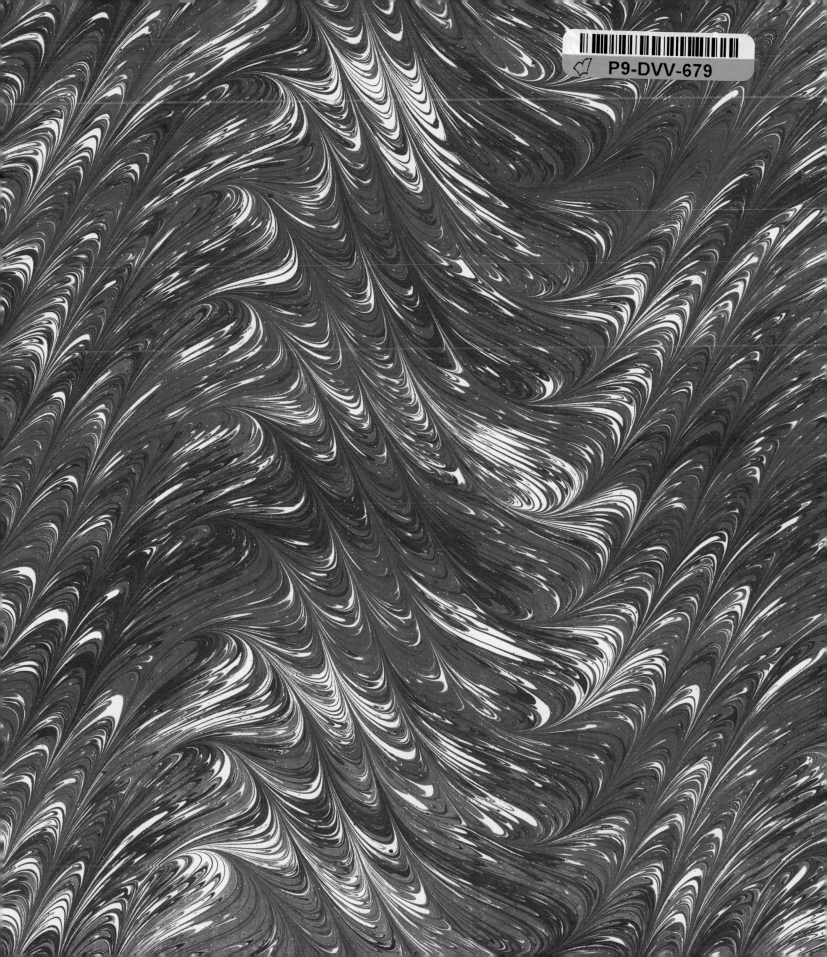

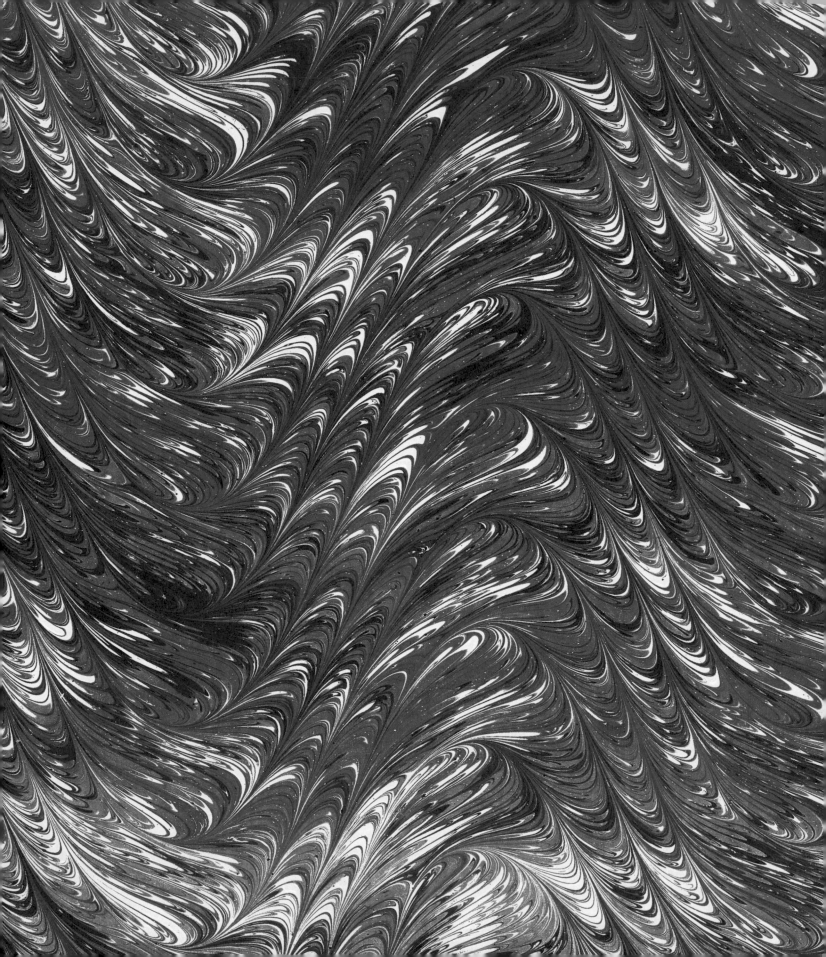

· TROPHIES ·

A HARCOURT READING/LANGUAGE ARTS PROGRAM

TIME TOGETHER

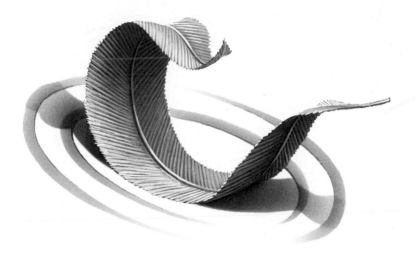

SENIOR AUTHORS
Isabel L. Beck ◆ Roger C. Farr ◆ Dorothy S. Strickland

AUTHORS
Alma Flor Ada ◆ Marcia Brechtel ◆ Margaret McKeown
Nancy Roser ◆ Hallie Kay Yopp

SENIOR CONSULTANT
Asa G. Hilliard III

CONSULTANTS
F. Isabel Campoy ◆ David A. Monti

Harcourt

Orlando   Boston   Dallas   Chicago   San Diego

Visit *The Learning Site!*

www.harcourtschool.com

Dear Reader,

Stories can be about so many things! This book has a mystery, a story about the future, and an interview with a real animal doctor. It also takes you inside a beehive to see what busy bees do there. There is so much to read and so much to learn! Enjoy your **Time Together** with these special stories.

Sincerely,

The Authors

The Authors

Hello, Neighbor

CONTENTS

Reading Across Texts

Theme Big Books

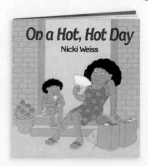

On a Hot, Hot Day
Nicki Weiss

Hattie and the Fox
by Mem Fox
Illustrated by Patricia Mullins

Decodable Books 19-26

DECODABLE BOOK 19

Hello, Neighbor

Word Power

Words to Remember

also

anything

know

moved

only

room

should

those

write

Lee's cat had kittens. I wanted one more than **anything**.

"If **only** I could have a kitten!" I said.

Lee said, "You **should** ask your mom."

I said, "I **know**! I will **write** her a letter."

She said I could have two! I picked a white kitten and **also** a black one. **Those** kittens **moved** into my **room** with me!

9

Award-
Winning
Author/
Illustrator

Genre

Realistic Fiction

Realistic fiction stories are made up, but they could happen in real life.

Look for:

- things that could really happen.

- characters that act like people you know.

A BED Full of CATS

by Holly Keller

12

Flora is Lee's cat. She is as soft as
silk. Flora sleeps on Lee's
bed. Lee likes it that way.

When Lee moves his feet under the quilt, Flora jumps on them. **Thump!** When Lee wiggles his fingers under the sheet, Flora tries to catch them. **Swish!**

When Lee pets her, Flora purrs. **Purrrrrr . . .**
When Lee sleeps, Flora sleeps, too.

One night Lee had a bad dream. He wanted Flora. She wasn't on his quilt.

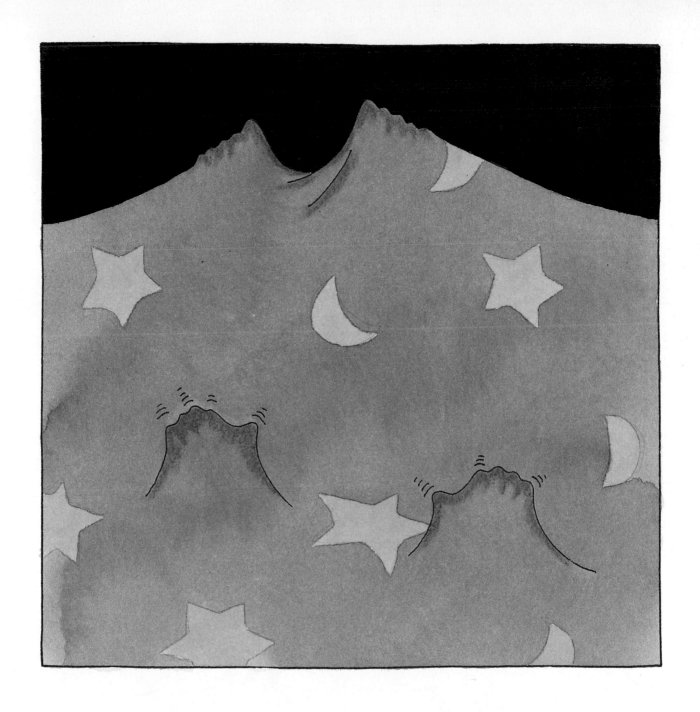

He moved his feet, but Flora didn't jump
on them. He wiggled his fingers, but Flora
didn't try to catch them. He wanted to
hear her purr, but Flora was not there.

The next day Flora was not in Lee's
room. She was not on Lee's bed. Lee
didn't know where Flora was.

"You should try to look for her," said Mama.

"We'll help you," Papa said.

"She'll come home when she needs to eat," said Grandma.

Lee looked for Flora in the house.

Mama looked all around the garden.

Papa looked in the trash bins.

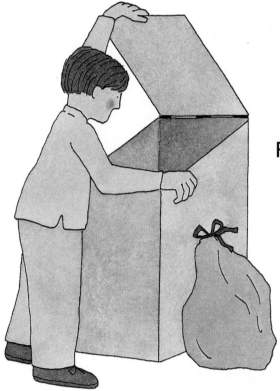

Grandma looked up in the peach trees.

20

Flora didn't come home. Lee was very sad.
His eyes were full of tears. If only Flora
would come back! "Please come home,"
Lee cried.

"We could put an ad in the newspaper,"
Papa said. "What should we write?"
"Write this," said Lee. "We lost our cat,
Flora. If you find her, please call. Then
give our number."

Lee didn't hear anything about Flora.
No one found Flora, and she didn't
come home. Days and weeks went by.

23

Then one night Lee felt something on his
bed. He moved his feet under the quilt.
Thump! Thump, thump, thump, thump!

He wiggled his fingers under the sheet.
Swish! Swish, swish, swish, swish!
Lee sat up and turned on his lamp.

There was Flora—with four kittens!
"Flora is home!" Lee yelled. "And
that's not all!"
Mama, Papa, and Grandma ran to
Lee's room.

Now Lee has a bed full of cats and he likes it that way. Those cats are as soft as silk. They are also fun.

Thump, thump.
Swish, swish.
Purrrrrr!

Think and Respond

1 Where did you think Flora was when she was missing?

2 What words does the author use to tell how Lee feels? Find them.

3 What would you have done if you were Lee and your pet was gone?

4 How would the story be different if Flora never came back?

5 What does the author do to make the end of the story a surprise?

Meet the Author/Illustrator

Holly Keller

Some of Holly Keller's ideas for this story came from things that her children did. When her children, Corey and Jesse, were little, they wouldn't sleep without their favorite stuffed animals on their beds. Corey's favorite stuffed animal was a mother cat with kittens, just like Flora in the story.

Teacher Read-Aloud
Poem

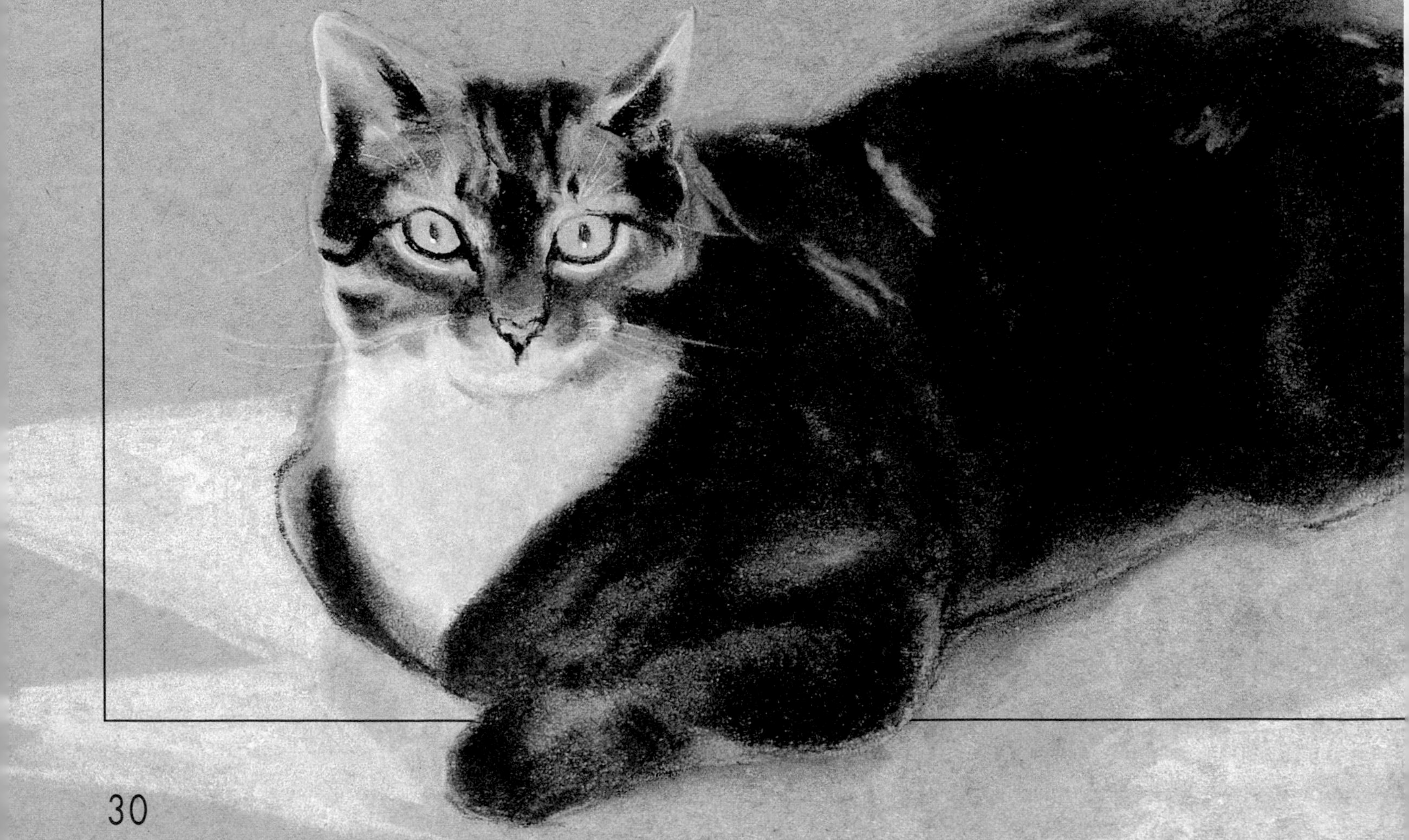

Our Cat

The cat goes out
And the cat comes back
And no one can follow
Upon her track.
She knows where she's going,
She knows where she's been,
And all we can do
Is to let her in.

by Marchette Chute
illustrated by Ed Young

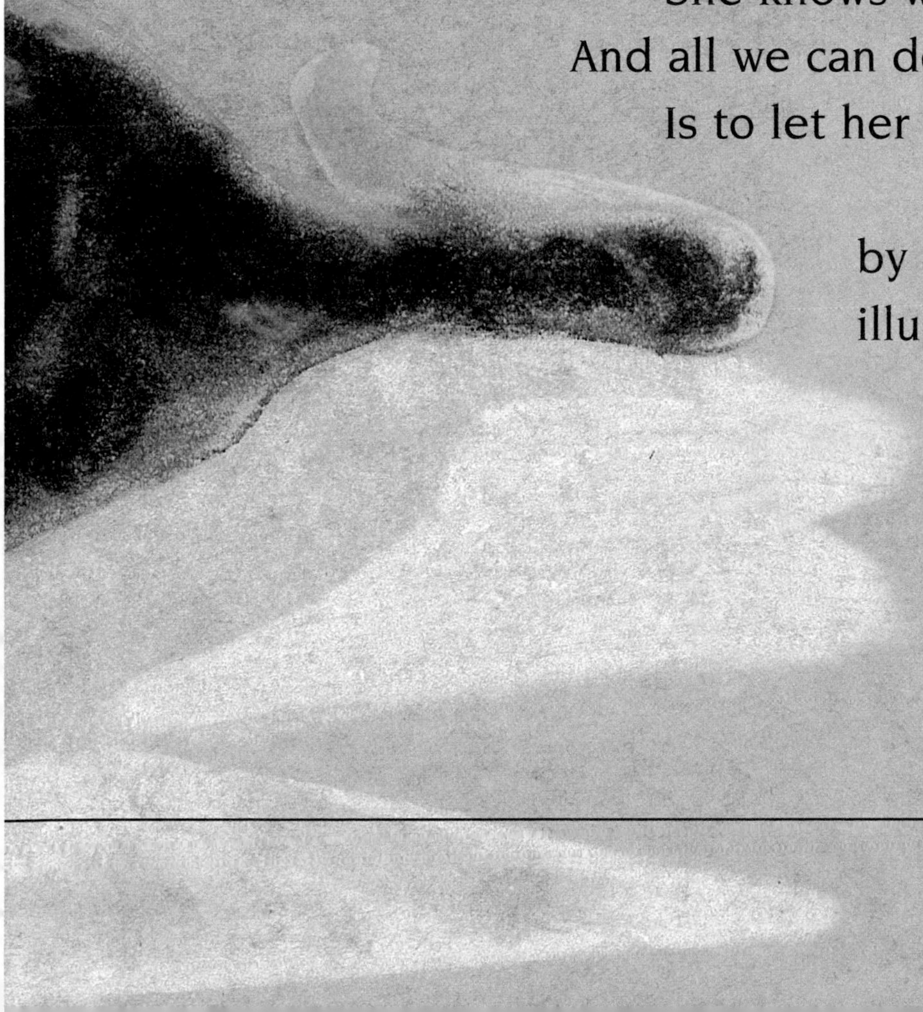

Making Connections

A Book Full of Pets

Choose a favorite kind of pet. Draw that animal, and write about why you like it. Add your work to a class book.

Writing
CONNECTION

I love dogs. They play with you and they are good friends. My dog licks my face all the time.

How Many Cats?

Now Lee has a bed full of cats! With Flora and her four kittens, how many cats are there in all?

Make up a cat math problem. Share your work.

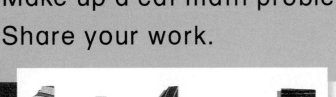

$$1 + 4 = 5$$

Care of Pets

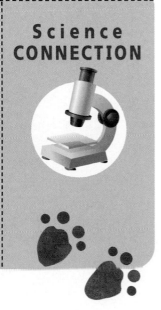

Talk about things you should do to take care of a pet. What should you feed the pet? How can you keep your pet safe and healthy? Make a poster of your ideas.

Alphabetize

Focus Skill

It is important to know **alphabetical order**, or ABC order. Words in a dictionary are in ABC order. Many lists of names are in ABC order, too.

Here are the names of three characters from "A Bed Full of Cats." Write these names in alphabetical order. Use the first letter of each name to put the names in order.

Papa   Lee   Mama

Test Prep
Alphabetize

1. **Which names are in alphabetical order?**
   ○ Jean, Carmen, Franklin
   ○ Franklin, Jean, Carmen
   ○ Carmen, Franklin, Jean

2. **Which names are in alphabetical order?**
   ○ Seth, Todd, Kim
   ○ Kim, Seth, Todd
   ○ Todd, Kim, Seth

Tip

Remember to use the first letter of each name to put the names in order.

Word Power

Words to Remember

country

Earth

over

special

town

world

We all live on **Earth**. My **country** is very **special** to me. So is the **town** where I live. One day I will go all **over** the **world**!

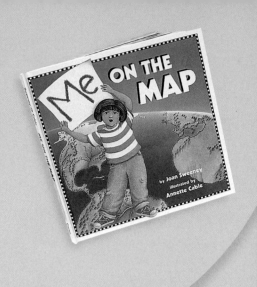

Genre

Nonfiction

In nonfiction, an author sometimes uses a character to give information.

Look for:

- a character who shares information.

- information about maps.

ON THE MAP

by Joan Sweeney

illustrated by
Annette Cable

This is me.
This is me in my room.

This is a map of my room.

This is me on the map of my room.

This is my house.

This is a map of my house.
This is my room on the map of my house.

This is my street.

This is a map of my street.
This is my house on the map of my street.

This is my town.

This is a map of my town.

This is my street on the map of my town.

This is my state.

This is a map of my state.

This is my town on the map of my state.

This is my country. The United States of America.

This is a map of my country.

This is my state on the map
of my country.

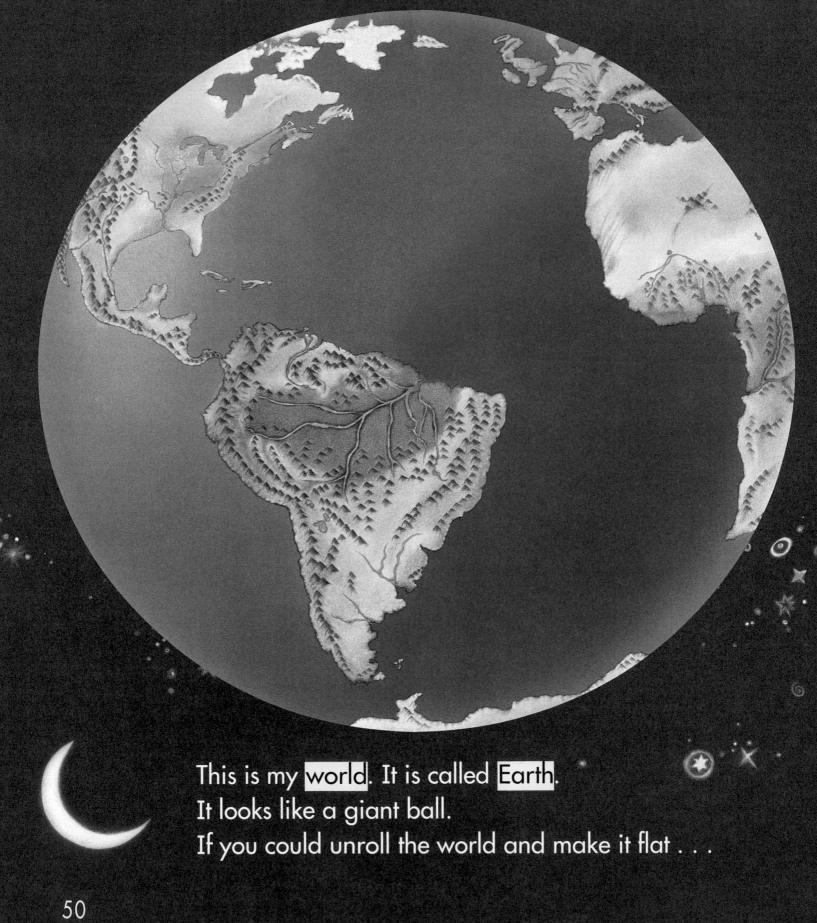

This is my world. It is called Earth.
It looks like a giant ball.
If you could unroll the world and make it flat . . .

. . . it would look something like this map of the world.

OUR WORLD

EUROPE

NORTH
AMERICA

ASIA

AFRICA

SOUTH
AMERICA

AUSTRALIA

ANTARCTICA

This is my country on the map of the world.

So here's how I find my special place on the map. First I look at the map of the world and find my country.

OUR WORLD

NORTH AMERICA

SOUTH AMERICA

EUROPE

ASIA

AUSTRALIA

ANTA

Then I look at the map of my country and find my state.
Then I look at the map of my state and find my town.

Then I look at the map of my town and find my street.

And on my street I find my house.

And in my house I find my room.
And in my room I find me!
Just think . . .

. . . in rooms, in houses, on streets,
in towns, in countries all **over** the world,
everybody has their own
special place on the map.

57

Just like me.
Just like me on the map.

Think and Respond

1 What did you learn from reading the story?

2 How do the words and pictures work together to give information?

3 Do you think maps are important? Explain your answer.

4 How could you use this story to make a map of your own?

5 How has this story changed the way you think about where you live?

Meet the Author

Joan Sweeney

Joan Sweeney wrote *Me on the Map* to help children learn about maps. She has written three other books, one about how the body works, one about space, and one about families.

 Visit *The Learning Site!*
www.harcourtschool.com

Joan Sweeney

Meet the Illustrator
Annette Cable

When Annette Cable was your age, she let people know what she was thinking by drawing pictures. She used real maps to help her draw the ones in *Me on the Map*. She wanted the maps to be just right, so she spent a lot of time drawing them.

Making Connections

Your Own Map!

Draw a map of a place that you know well. Share your map. Tell why you chose that place.

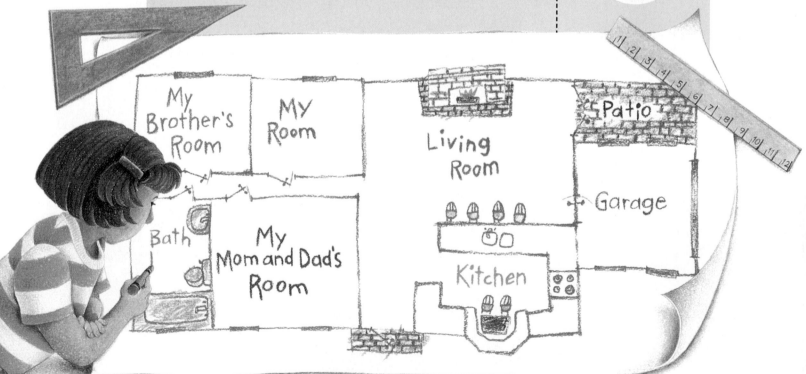

A Great Place to Visit

Look at a map or globe. Choose a place you would like to visit. Draw what the place might look like. Write about it.

States and Their Neighbors

Find your state on a map. Work with others to answer these questions.

- How many other states are next to your state? What are they?
- Is your state next to either Mexico or Canada?

Classify/Categorize

Noticing how things are alike can help you when you read. Look at these pictures from "Me on the Map."

• What does each picture show?
• How are the pictures all alike?

Now read these words from the story. Tell how these things are alike.

| state | country | town |

Test Prep
Classify/Categorize

1. How are these things alike?

corn   beans   peach

○ All are animals.

○ All are foods.

○ All are places to live.

2. How are these alike?

frog   rabbit   pig

○ All are games.

○ All are places
   to live.

○ All are animals.

Tip

Read all three words
and picture each thing
in your mind before
you answer.

Word Power

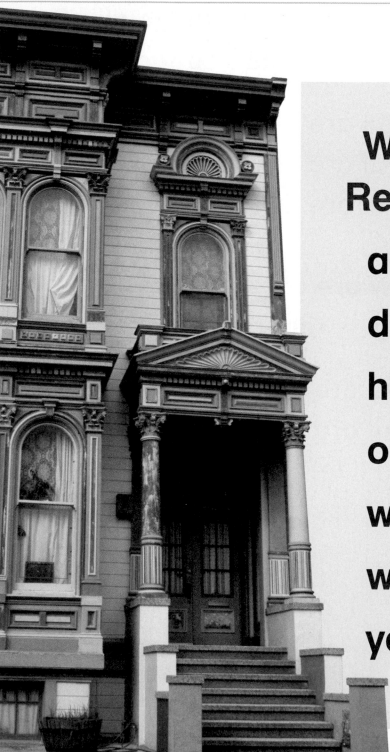

**Words to
Remember**

above

different

hold

old

warm

water

years

This kind of house can **hold** lots of people. It's **different** than our **old** house. We have lived here for two **years**. My friend Jack and his family live **above** us. The park near us has a pond. On **warm** days, Jack and I play by the **water**.

AT HOME AROUND THE WORLD

by Lucy Floyd

All people need shelter. Shelters
give us safety and a place to rest. A
house is a shelter.

A house can be big or small. It can be tall and skinny or low and boxy.

What kind of house would you like best?

71

Some houses are new. Other houses are very old. They have been standing in the same spot for years and years.

Some houses are for one or two people. Lots of people live in apartment houses!

Houses in different parts of the world
are different. In hot lands, houses need
to keep out the sun and let in a breeze.

In frosty lands, houses are shelters
from wind and snow. They help people
keep warm.

People make shelters from things around them. They can use trees or branches. They can use mud, rocks, or grass.

People have made shelters from cloth, animal hair, and blocks of snow!

77

This is a tepee. It is made with animal skins. The people who made tepees were hunters. They needed homes that were easy to take with them on a hunt.

Other people made homes that would last. Some houses could hold only one family. Other houses were made to hold lots of people.

In hot places, people baked clay bricks in the sun. Then they made houses with the bricks.

In the far north, people made shelters from big blocks of snow! People there still use these shelters on hunting trips.

People made houses from other things, too.

Some people made houses out of dirt and grass. They called them sod houses. What do you think they did when it rained?

Some houses today are like houses from the past. In the sandy desert, some people live in tents. Others make houses with clay bricks. Thick walls keep out the sand and sun.

This house sits up on stilts. The stilts keep
the house above water.

Some people live in houses that float! This boat is called a junk. In the past, junks were floating homes. They still are today.

Lots of people like to live on the water.

This is a house on wheels. It can stop in one spot or move on. It has many things you can find in a house.

All around the world,
we see all sorts of houses!

Think about your own dream house. What will it be?

THINK AND RESPOND

1. What is the main thing this selection tells about houses?

2. Do you think the author likes writing about houses? Tell why or why not.

3. Why is it a good idea for people to build houses from things around them, such as clay or rocks?

4. Why was a tepee a good home for people who moved around a lot?

5. Which house in the selection would you most like to live in? Why?

LUCY FLOYD

Lucy Floyd

Lucy Floyd was once a teacher. She thought about how children like to make houses out of big boxes when she wrote "At Home Around the World." She says, "Houses are interesting. They come in all shapes, sizes and colors." Lucy Floyd lives in a pink house in Cambridge, Massachusetts.

91

Our Homes

Foxes live in dirt holes. This fennec fox lives in a hole in the desert. He keeps cool by staying underground for most of the day.

Cougar cubs live in rock holes. They have spotted fur. Their fur blends with the rock. This keeps them safe. Enemies have a hard time seeing them.

Are Holes

Owls live in tree holes. This screech owl is looking to see "whoo-whoo" is taking her picture. She naps during the day in her hole. At night she hunts squirrels.

Mother polar bears live in snow holes with their cubs. A mother bear digs a hole before her cubs are born. When she gives birth, her cubs stay warm. Thick snow keeps out icy winds.

93

Making Connections

Dream Houses

What would your dream house be like? Draw a picture of it. Write about your dream house. Share your work with others.

Writing
CONNECTION

My dream house is a castle.

Build a House

Art
Make a little house. It can be like a house you just read about, or it can be different. Tell about your house.

Art CONNECTION

From Soil to Bricks

Some people make bricks for houses by baking clay in the sun. Mix a little water into some clay or another kind of soil. Form it into a brick shape and let it dry. What happens?

Science CONNECTION

Classify/Categorize

Focus
Skill

Putting things into groups can help
you organize your thoughts as
you read.

Look at these pictures from
"At Home Around the World."
What groups do they belong in?

Visit *The Learning Site!*
www.harcourtschool.com
See *Skills* and *Activities*

Test Prep
Classify/Categorize

1. **Which group of words belongs together?**

   ○ apartment   house   apple
   ○ apartment   tent   house
   ○ beach   tent   house

2. **Which group of words belongs together?**

   ○ warm   clock   cold
   ○ hot   warm   bird
   ○ cold   hot   warm

Tip

Read each group of words. Is there one thing that's the same about all three?

▲ Tell Me a Story

Word Power

Words to Remember

because

cook

front

listen

most

picture

why

young

I like to **listen** to Abuelita **most** of all.
I'll tell you **why**.
It's **because** Abuelita tells great
stories!
Sometimes she tells them as we **cook**
together.
Sometimes I just sit in **front** of her and
listen.
I like to **picture** what she was like
when she was **young**.

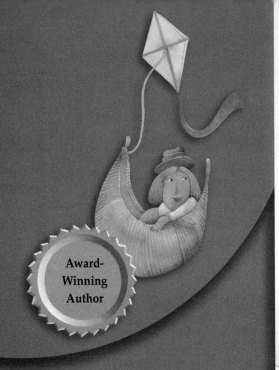

Genre

Fiction

In fiction, an author can tell a story through dialogue—or what the characters say to each other.

Look for:

- Information that one character tells another character.

- Clues to the characters' ideas in the words and in the pictures.

100

Tell Me a Story

by Alma Flor Ada

illustrated by Gerardo Suzán

"Tell me a story, Abuelita," said Camila.
"Tell me a story about long ago."

"What would you like to hear? Would you
like to hear about your father when he
was a young man?"

"No, Abuelita. Tell me about when you were a little girl."

103

"Listen, Camila, and I will tell you. When I was a little girl, my family did not own a car. We didn't ride places. We walked."

"That must have been hard, Abuelita. Did you stop to rest a lot?"

"It was fine, Camila. Walking is fun."

"Tell me more, Abuelita."

"We didn't have many of the things we have today. We had to use coal to cook."

"Did you cook with coal every day?"

"Of course we did, Camila. We had to cook
every day, and we used coal."

107

"My friends and I had such fun! We played
outside in front of the house. We liked to
jump rope on the sidewalk."

"Why did you play in front of the house, Abuelita?"

"We played there because it was the best place to play, Camila."

"What did you like most when you were young, Abuelita?"

"I liked flying kites. On windy days, the kites went so far up it was hard to see them. I let my dreams fly with the kites."

110

"I can picture all the kites! I would let my dreams fly up with kites, too!"

"What I liked most of all was the river in back of *my* Abuelita's house."

"The river, Abuelita? Why did you like the river?"

"There was a big tree at the side of the river. I would sit on a branch and look down. I could see ducks, fish, and bullfrogs. I kept looking for a crocodile, but all I saw were turtles."

"Bullfrogs? Didn't they scare you, Abuelita?"

"Oh, no, Camila. It was fun. I had the best time at the river."

"I made boats and sent them down the river. I would picture them landing on a beautiful island. I wished I could sail with them. I wished I could sail all the way to the sea."

"Weren't you scared, Abuelita?"

"No, Camila, I don't think so."

"I would sail with you, Abuelita! I
wouldn't be scared!"

"I think we will sail, Camila. One day, we will sail."

116

Think and Respond

1. What does Abuelita share with Camila?

2. For each story Abuelita shares, there are two pictures. How are those two pictures different?

3. How did Abuelita go from place to place when she was young?

4. Does Camila enjoy listening to Abuelita? How do you know?

5. Which of Abuelita's stories do you like best? Why?

Meet the Author

Alma Flor Ada

Alma Flor Ada comes from a family that loves to tell stories. As a child, she listened to her father, uncles, and grandmother tell wonderful tales. She wrote "Tell Me a Story" about her own granddaughter, Camila. Whenever she sees Camila, the first thing Camila says is "Tell me a story, Abuelita!"

Alma Flor Ada says, "My granddaughter always asks for *real* stories. I always wonder what Camila is imagining as I tell her my stories. I hope this story helps you wonder about the past, too."

Alma Flor Ada

Meet the Illustrator
Gerardo Suzán

Gerardo Suzán was born in Mexico City, Mexico. Now he lives in Torreón, near the desert where his ancestors lived long ago. Gerardo Suzán has illustrated more than fifty books for children. He says, "I like blue skies with a bright sun shining and I include them in my illustrations whenever possible."

G. Suzán

Making Connections

Your Own Family Story

Ask an older family member to tell you a story about when he or she was young. Compare that story with your life now. Share what you learn.

Social Studies CONNECTION

120

Sail Away

Where should Abuelita and Camila go on their sailing trip? Draw and write a story about them. Add it to a class book of sailing stories.

Writing CONNECTION

Sailing with Camila and Abuelita

Bullfrogs: Scary or Not?

How does Camila picture the bullfrogs Abuelita talks about? Find out something about real bullfrogs. Share what you learn.

Science/ Technology CONNECTION

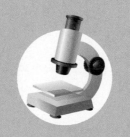

Alphabetize

A B C D E F G H I J K

You have read stories by authors Holly Keller, Lucy Floyd, and Alma Flor Ada. In a library, books are in alphabetical order by their last names. Put their names in ABC order. Use the first letter of the last name.

Keller, Holly
Floyd, Lucy
Ada, Alma Flor

L M N O P Q R S T U V W X Y Z

122

Test Prep
Alphabetize

1. **Which last names are in alphabetical order?**
    - ○ Sanchez, Ling, Gorman
    - ○ Gorman, Ling, Sanchez
    - ○ Ling, Gorman, Sanchez

2. **Which last names are in alphabetical order?**
    - ○ Miller, Dorn, Wu
    - ○ Dorn, Miller, Wu
    - ○ Wu, Dorn, Miller

Tip

Look at the first letter in each name. Then look at an ABC chart. Does the order match?

Word Power

▲ My Robot

Words to Remember

almost

always

does

even

once

pretty

say

sound

Cecil is my friend. He is **almost always** with me. He makes a funny **sound** when he moves.

Cecil **does** a lot to help me.

He **even** cooked my dinner **once**!

He makes **pretty** cakes, too!

I **say** I am lucky to have Cecil.

Who is Cecil? You'll find out.

Award-Winning Author

Genre

Science Fiction

In science fiction, things happen that can't happen yet but MAY happen in the future.

Look for:

- Tools and machines that are different than tools we use today.

- Things that are the same as things today.

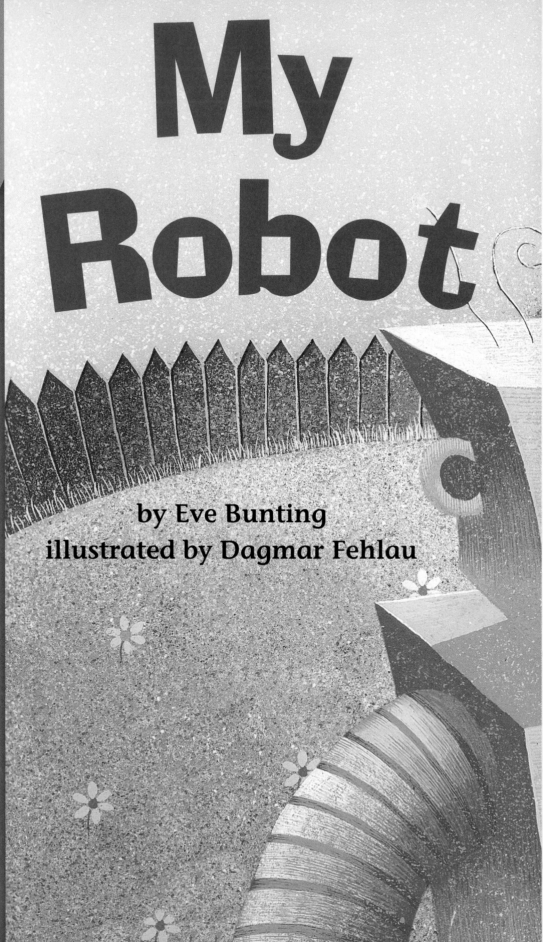

My Robot

by Eve Bunting
illustrated by Dagmar Fehlau

126

127

I got a new robot for my birthday. I call him Cecil. Ever since I got him, we have been doing lots of things together.

Cecil plays tag with the children at school.
WHIR! WHIR! We hear the sound of his
wheels spinning as he races after us.
Sometimes he goes a little too fast.

CRASH! SMASH!
Cecil hits the fence.
"Not the fence, Cecil!" I call. It's hard not
to laugh. Playing tag is not the best thing
my robot can do.

All my friends at school like Cecil a lot. He helps our teacher, Mr. Spencer. Helping Mr. Spencer is not the best thing my robot can do.

Cecil leads the school band.
RUM-A-TUM-TUM. Hear that drum.
"Don't dance, Cecil!" I say. "Don't
prance! Just march!"
The children in the band march along
after him. Leading the band is not the
best thing my robot can do.

Cecil picks me up after school.
He gives me a ride home.
"How's the weather up there?"
my little brother Dennis asks.
He gets a ride home, too.

134

Once in a while, Cecil does tricks with our dog.
They can roll over. WHIRL! WHIRL!
They can beg. CREAK! FIZZ! WHIZ!
"Shake, Prince," says Dennis.
"Shake, Cecil," he says.
Doing tricks is not the best thing my robot
can do.

135

Cecil plays hide-and-seek, too. He is always IT. He gives everyone a chance to find a good place to hide.

CLANK! CLUNK! Here comes Cecil!
We don't say we heard him coming. He
whistles when he finds us. WHIR! SPARK!
POP! Playing hide-and-seek is not the best
thing my robot can do.

137

Everyone has heard about Cecil's cakes.
He makes circus animals with the frosting.
His cakes are almost too pretty to eat.
"This is your best cake yet!" says Dennis.

"Cecil's cakes are pretty good," I say , "but that is still not the best thing my robot can do."

"My tummy tells me it is," Dennis says.

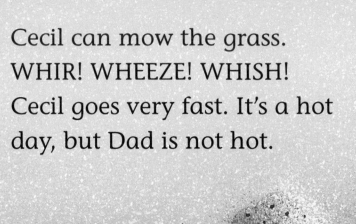

Cecil can mow the grass.
WHIR! WHEEZE! WHISH!
Cecil goes very fast. It's a hot
day, but Dad is not hot.

"This <u>must</u> be the best thing Cecil can do," says Dad.

"Almost," I tell Dad. "You and Dennis come with me. I'll show you something else Cecil can do."

"Look in here. Even cleaning my room is not the best thing my robot can do." I give Cecil a hug.

"Thanks, Cecil," I whisper. "The very best thing you can do is be my friend!"

FLASH! SPARK! WHIRL! POP!
Cecil knows.

Think and Respond

1 What does Cecil do for the boy in the story?

2 If you had a robot, what would you want your robot to do for you?

3 How can you tell that Cecil is a good friend?

4 What do the pictures tell you about when this story takes place?

5 Would you rather live now or in the time of the story? Tell why.

Meet the Author

Eve Bunting

Dear Boys and Girls,

I once met a robot. Students had made him out of cardboard. He was a great robot! Each of the boys and girls took him home for one night.

I thought about how grand it would be to have my very own robot. So I wrote a story about one and called it "My Robot." I am happy to share it with you.

Eve Bunting

Meet the Illustrator
Dagmar Fehlau

Dear Boys and Girls,

I was born in Germany, and then I came to the United States to study art. I always loved drawing and painting, so I knew I would be an artist when I grew up. When I finished school, I began to do illustration work. I hope you like the pictures in "My Robot."

Dagmar Fehlau

Visit *The Learning Site!*
www.harcourtschool.com

145

Visit the Robot Zoo

The Body Works Issue

chickaDEE

Get in the Swim with a visit to the Robot Zoo

PLUS
Slalom Thrills and Spills, and more!

Stroke!

Polar bear

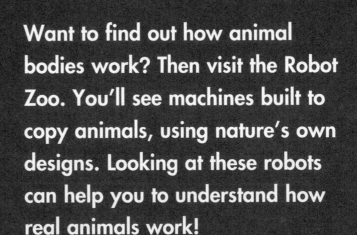

Want to find out how animal bodies work? Then visit the Robot Zoo. You'll see machines built to copy animals, using nature's own designs. Looking at these robots can help you to understand how real animals work!

Look Up

The giraffe has a very long neck. But it only has seven neck bones, the same as a person. They're just each a foot long! The robot giraffe has a metal framework to hold up its neck and a big piston that works like the giraffe's strong neck muscle.

147

Buzz Off

A house fly is so hard to swat because both of its eyes have about 4,000 six-sided lenses. They help the fly see just about everything!

Take Off

Grasshoppers can hop and fly. So this robot has powerful springs in its two rear legs that work like the rear-leg muscles in a real grasshopper. Its muscles help it fly up, up, and away!

Making Connections

Robot Puppets

Make a robot stick puppet. Act out ways your robot could help you.

Art CONNECTION

My Robot Wish

Think of one thing you would like to have a robot do for you. Draw and write about it. Share your work.

My robot plays catch with me.

Robots on the Job

Real robots do jobs that are hard for people to do. Find out how real robots help people in their work. Share what you learn.

151

When c Sounds Like s
Phonics Skill

Sometimes the letter c stands for the sound for s. You hear this sound twice in Cecil.

Read these words from the story. What sound does the letter c stand for?

Cecil	races	dance
place	fence	since

Point to the letter that comes after the c in each word. If the letter i or e comes after the c, the c usually stands for the sound for s.

Now read these words. In which words does the c stand for the sound for s?

pencil pickle city candy

Test Prep
When c Sounds Like s

1. **In which group of words does c stand for the sound for s?**
   - ○ act   cart   cake
   - ○ face   force   race
   - ○ can   pack   coat
   - ○ chug   cup   track

2. **In which group of words does c stand for the sound for s?**
   - ○ cat   cuddle   correct
   - ○ tack   case   cot
   - ○ can   pack   coat
   - ○ prince   ace   trace

Tip

Look for the letters i or e after the c. Then read the words and listen for the sound for s.

153

Word Power

Words to Remember

any

Dr.

busy

care

eight

took

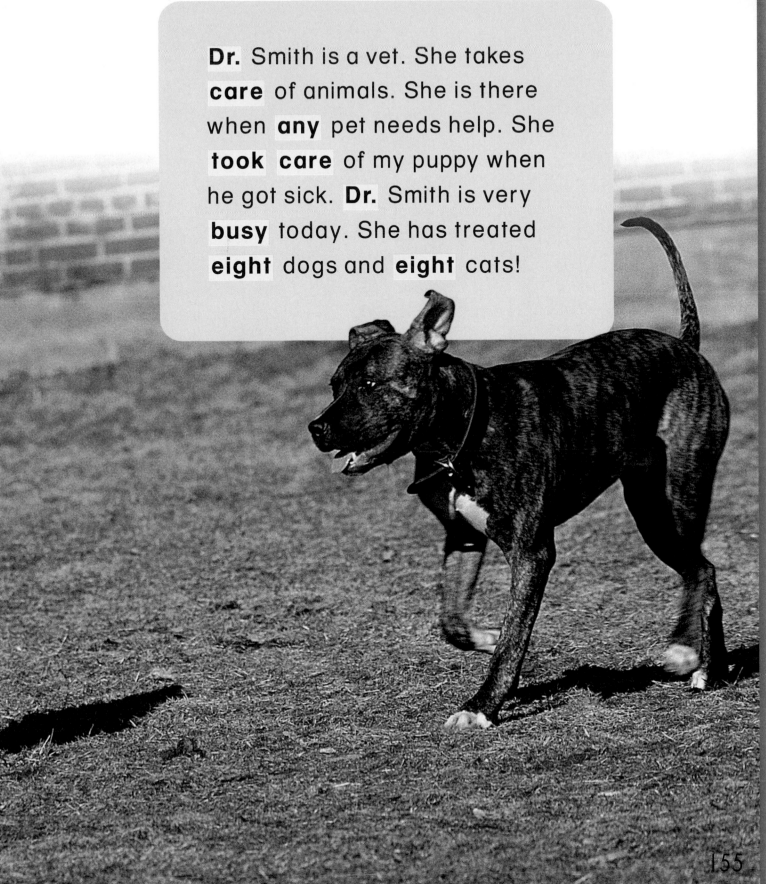

Dr. Smith is a vet. She takes **care** of animals. She is there when **any** pet needs help. She **took** **care** of my puppy when he got sick. **Dr.** Smith is very **busy** today. She has treated **eight** dogs and **eight** cats!

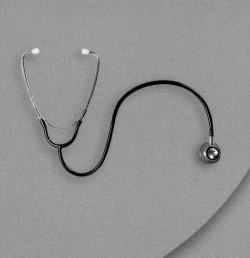

Genre

Nonfiction

Sometimes an author interviews a person to get information to share.

Look for:

- **Questions and answers.**
- **Information about a vet's work at an animal shelter.**

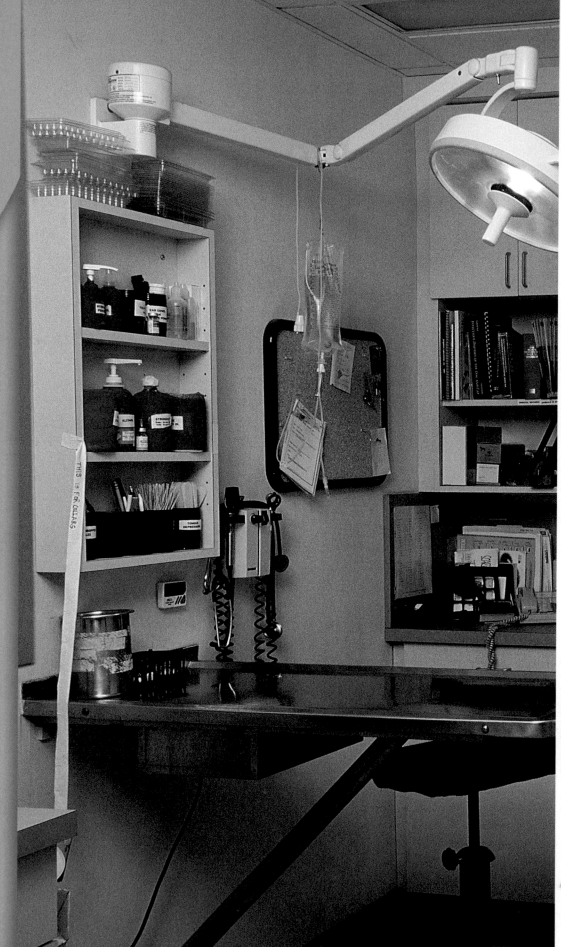

On the Job with
Dr. Martha Smith

by Claire Daniel
photographs by Rick Friedman

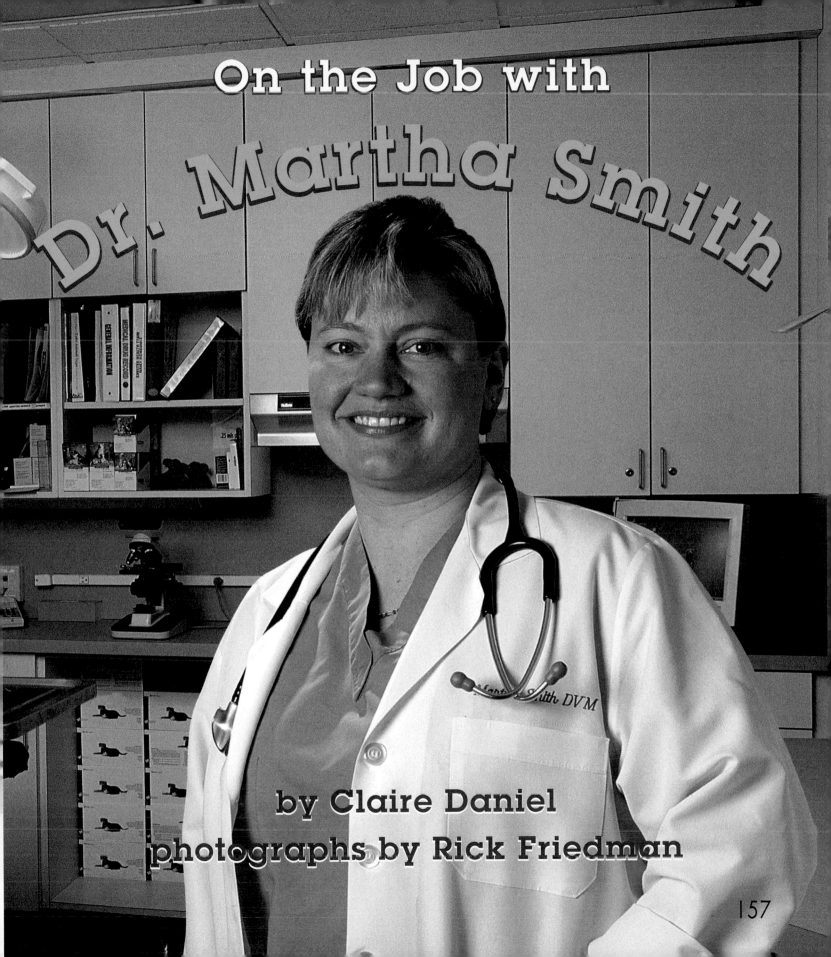

Dr. Martha Smith is a vet at an animal shelter.

Dr. Smith: Hi! You picked a good day to come. We will be busy! We have twenty new animals today.

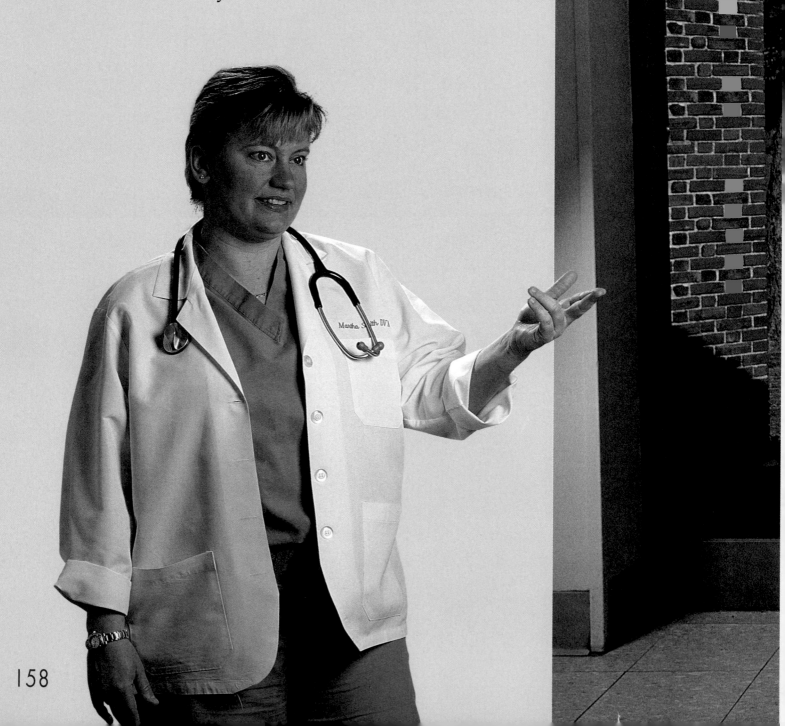

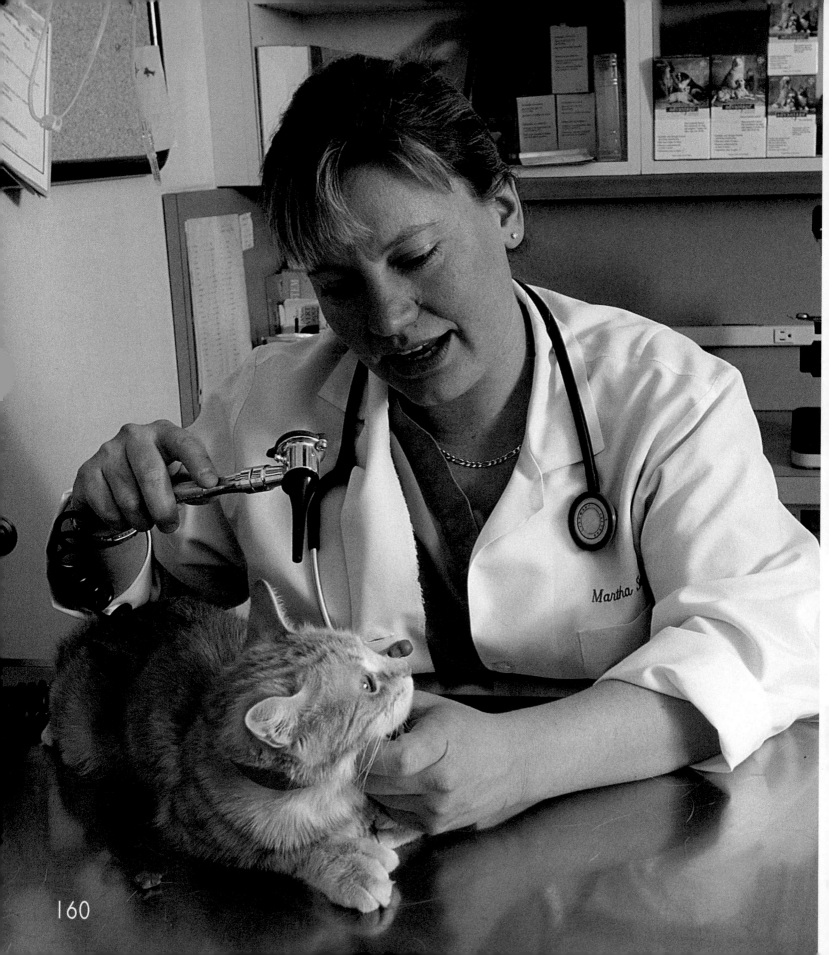

160

CD: What do you do first each day?

Dr. Smith: I check to see if any of the new animals are sick. I look at their eyes and ears. Sometimes I give them shots. Come and meet a special cat.

161

CD: Will she find a home?

Dr. Smith: Read her story. See what you think.

Muffin

I was a lost kitty. A man found me and fed me. Then he took me to this shelter. I am a sweet cat. Will you please take me home with you?

Thank you,

Muffin

163

Dr. Smith: I wish I could spend time with Muffin, but I have to check the new animals.

Dr. Smith heard loud barking outside.
She went to see what was going on.

A worker was leading two dogs into the shelter.
"Come, Puffy. Come, Jake."

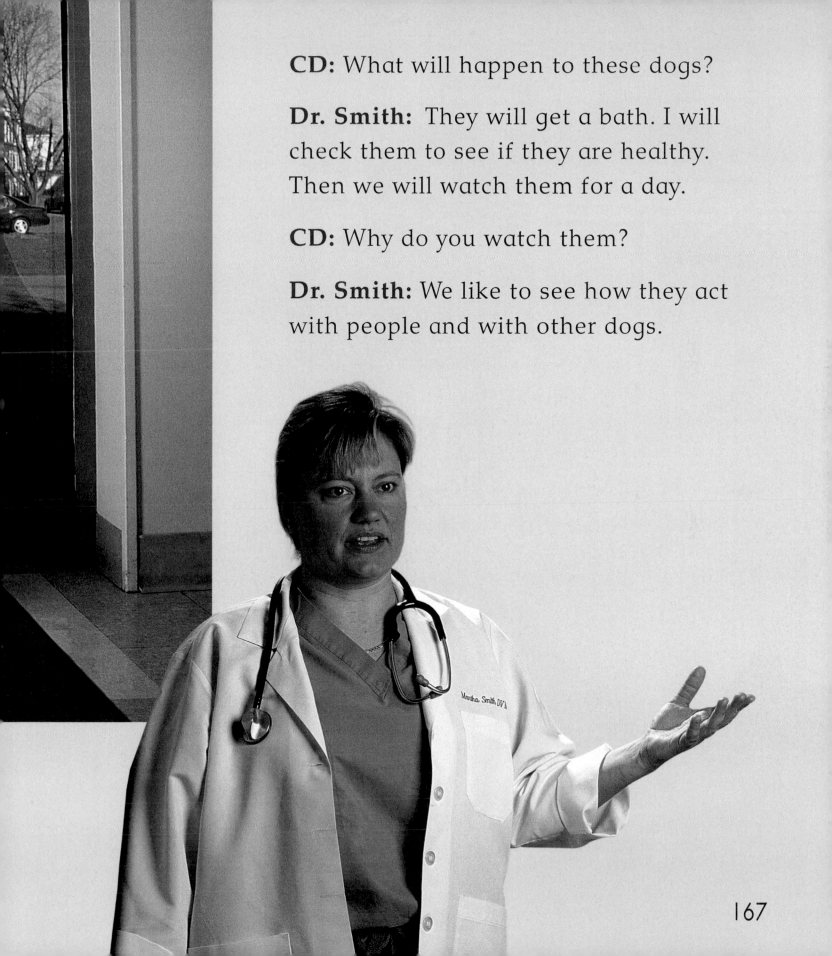

CD: What will happen to these dogs?

Dr. Smith: They will get a bath. I will check them to see if they are healthy. Then we will watch them for a day.

CD: Why do you watch them?

Dr. Smith: We like to see how they act with people and with other dogs.

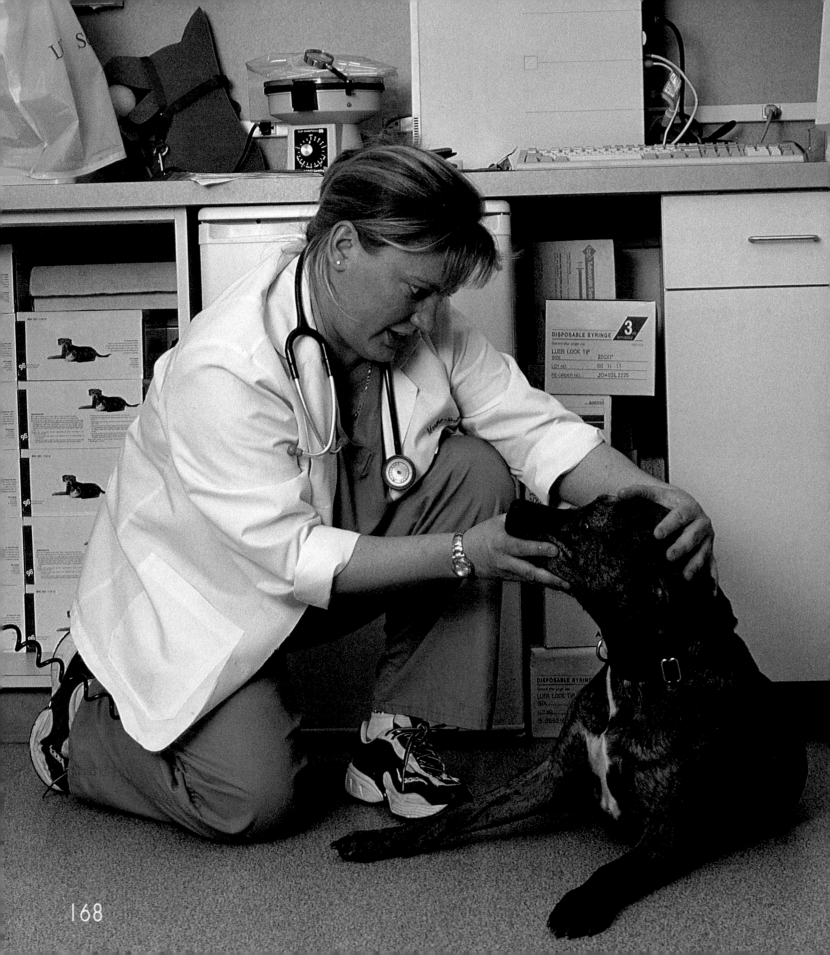

After lunch, Puffy and Jake were clean. Dr. Smith checked their fur for fleas and sores.

Dr. Smith: Jake is fine, but Puffy is sick. I will treat her. She will need time to heal. Puffy and Jake are great dogs. It's a shame about Puffy.

169

CD: Which animals do you see the most?

Dr. Smith: We get more cats than anything. We also get a lot of dogs and rabbits.

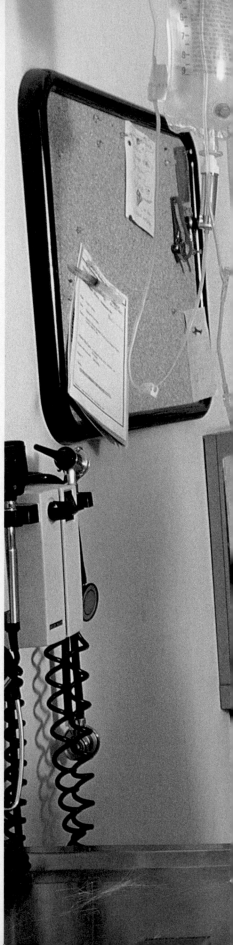

171

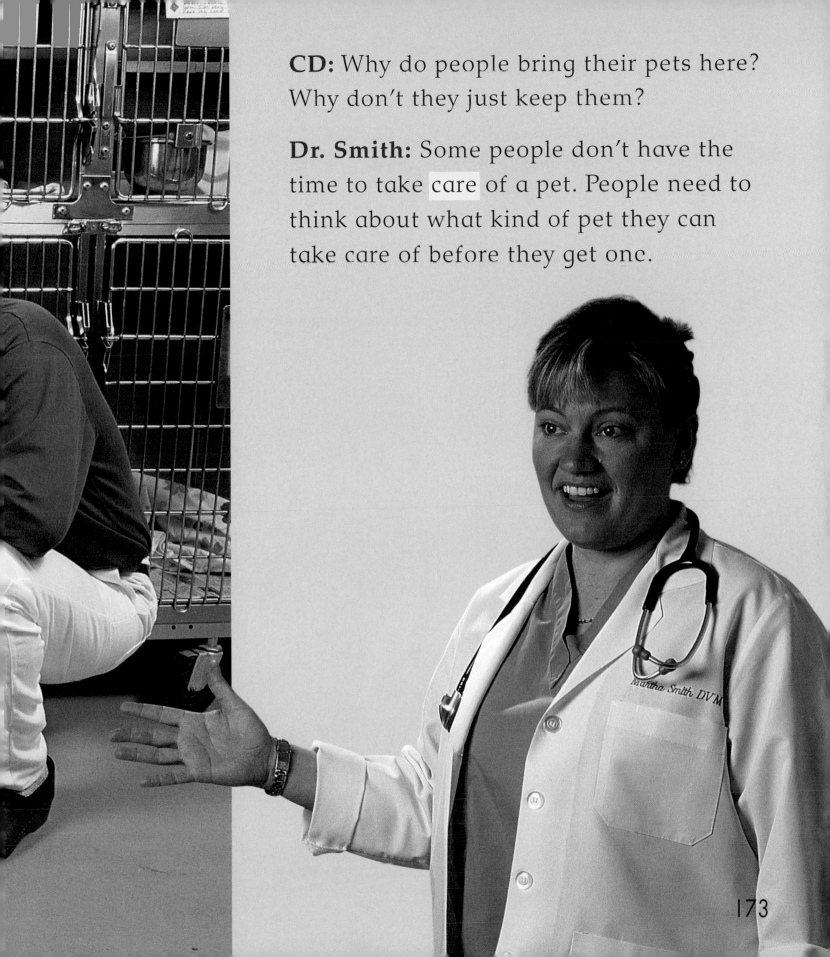

CD: Why do people bring their pets here? Why don't they just keep them?

Dr. Smith: Some people don't have the time to take care of a pet. People need to think about what kind of pet they can take care of before they get one.

173

It was 6:00. I thanked Dr. Smith. She said she would call me in eight weeks to tell me about Puffy and the animals. This is what we said.

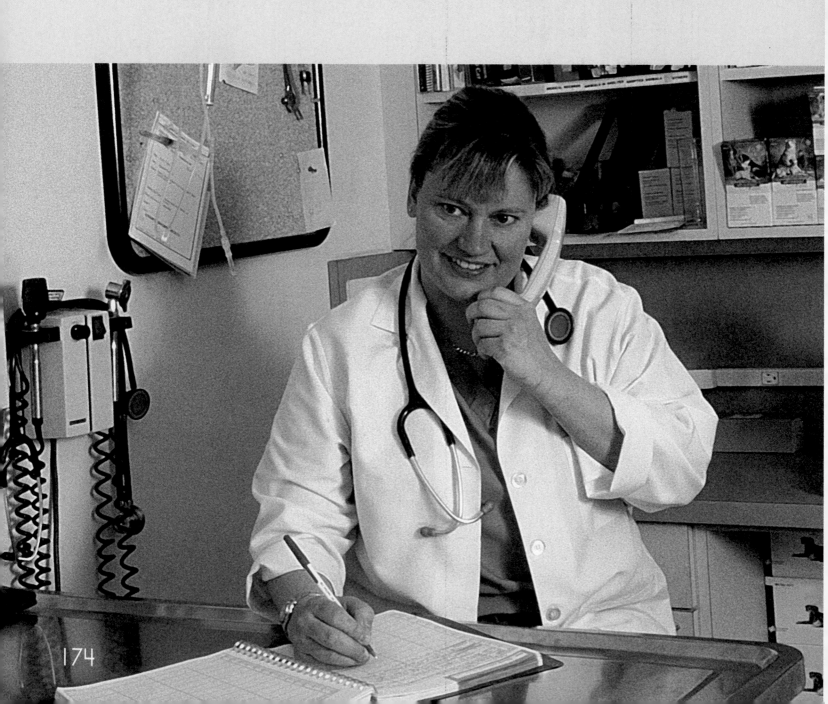

Dr. Smith: I have good news. A man adopted Jake two days after you left.

CD: That's wonderful! What happened to Muffin?

Dr. Smith: She left the same day I saw you.

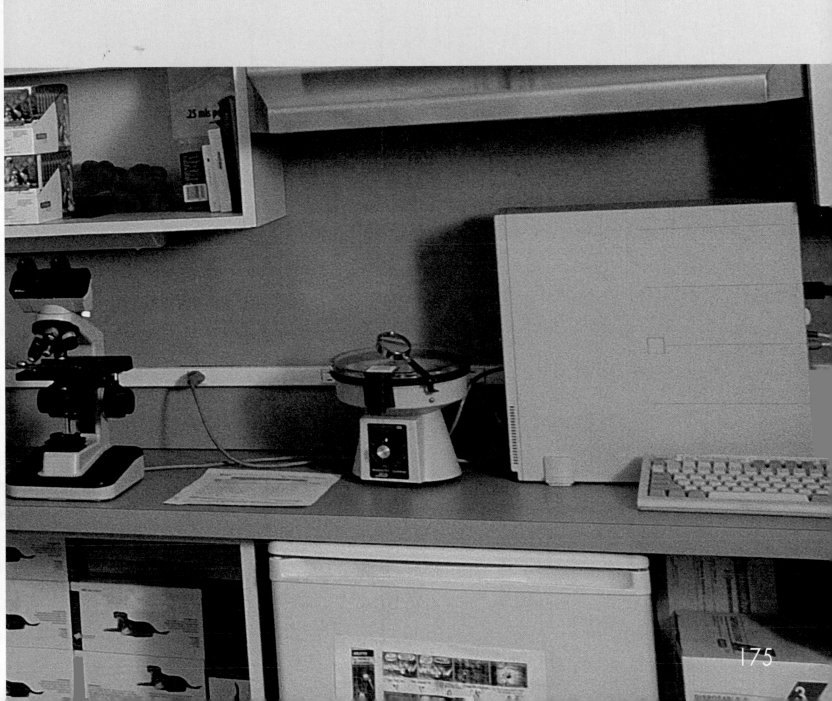

CD: I'm glad about Jake and Muffin! How is Puffy?

Dr. Smith: Puffy is much better! She is as strong as Jake now. The best news is that Jake's owner called, looking for a new pet. He is going to take Puffy! Now Puffy and Jake can be together!

177

Think and Respond

1. What does Dr. Smith do for the animals at the shelter?

2. Did Muffin really write her own story? Explain.

3. Do you think Puffy and Jake will be happy in their new home? Why?

4. Would you like to be a vet? Why or why not?

5. How does the author let Dr. Smith tell her own story?

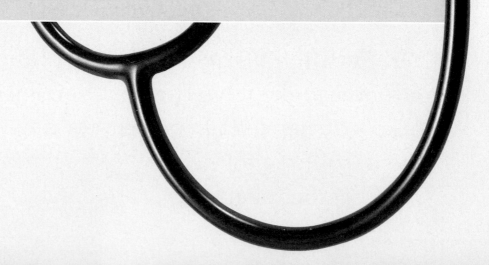

Meet the Author

Claire Daniel

Claire Daniel's favorite things to do are writing, traveling, taking photographs, and walking with her dogs. She has two Labrador retrievers. Their names are Gus and Oscar. She once took Oscar to Italy for three months!

Dr. Smith used to be Oscar's vet. Claire Daniel has written about her for a newspaper. Now she has helped you learn about her work. Claire Daniel misses having Dr. Smith as her vet, but she knows that Dr. Smith's work at the shelter is very important.

Claire Daniel

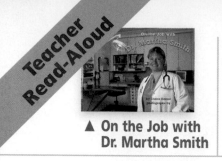
Making Connections

Your Own Animal Story

Pretend you are an animal at the shelter. Write about yourself. Use Muffin's story to get ideas.

Writing
CONNECTION

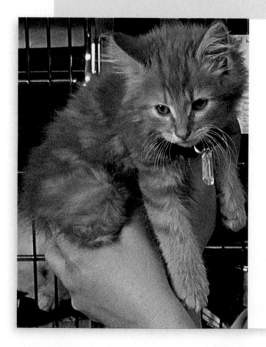

Muffin

I was a lost kitty. A man found me and fed me. Then he took me to this shelter. I am a sweet cat. Will you please take me home with you?

Thank you,

Muffin

How Many Animals?

Math
CONNECTION

Make up math problems like this one. Then trade problems with a friend.

Dr. Smith treated 8 cats and 4 rabbits. How many animals did she treat in all?

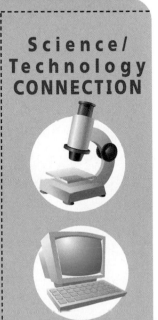

Healthy Pets

Science/
Technology
CONNECTION

What should you feed a pet?

Find out what dogs, cats, or other animals should eat to stay healthy. Share what you learn.

Classify/Categorize

Focus Skill

Thinking about ways in which things are alike can help you understand what you read. Here are three jobs workers do at the animal shelter. How are all these jobs alike?

check eyes and ears

give shots

give baths

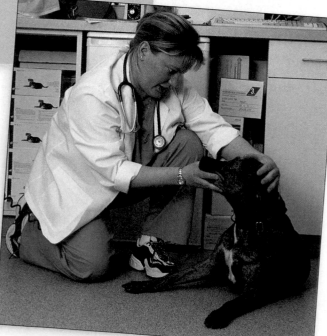

Visit *The Learning Site!*
www.harcourtschool.com

See *Skills* and *Activities*

182

Test Prep
Classify/Categorize

Things We Do

solve math problems

write stories

read books

I. How are all these things alike?

○ You do them all when you swim.

○ You do them all in school.

○ You do them all when you play ball.

Tip

Read the list and the choices carefully. Decide what is the same about the items in the list.

▲ Little Bear's Friend

Word Power

Words to Remember

again

blue

hello

high

love

opened

High up in the tree, I **opened** my eyes.
I **love** to see birds in the **blue** sky.
"**Hello**," said the birds.
"It's nice to see you **again**."

Genre

Fantasy

Characters in fantasy stories do impossible things.

Look for:

- **People talking to animals.**

- **Animals wearing clothes.**

LITTLE BEAR'S FRIEND

by ELSE HOLMELUND MINARIK

pictures by MAURICE SENDAK
by the author and artist of LITTLE BEAR

An I CAN READ Book®

Little Bear and Emily

Little Bear sat in the top
of a high tree.
He looked all about him
at the wide, wide world.

He saw the green hills.

He saw the river.

And far, far away

he saw the blue sea.

He saw the tops of trees.

He saw his own house.

He saw Mother Bear.

He could hear the wind sing.

And he could feel the wind

on his fur, on his eyes,

on his little black nose.

He shut his eyes,

and let the wind brush him.

He opened his eyes,

and saw two little squirrels.

"Play with us," they said.

"No time," said Little Bear.

"I have to go home for lunch."

He began to climb down,

and saw four little birds.

"Look at us," they said,

"we can fly."

"I can, too," said Little Bear,

"but I always fly down.

I can't fly up

or sideways."

He climbed down some more,

and saw a little green worm.

"Hello," said the little green worm.

"Talk to me."

"Some other time," said Little Bear.

"I have to go home for lunch."

He climbed all the way down,

and there he saw a little girl.

"I think I am lost,"
said the little girl.
"Could you see the river
from the treetop?"

"Oh, yes," said Little Bear,

"I could see the river.

Do you live there?"

"Yes," said the little girl.

"My name is Emily.

And this is my doll Lucy."

"I am Little Bear, and
I can take you to the river.
What is in that basket?"

"Cookies," said Emily. "Have some."

"Thank you. I love cookies."

"So do I," said Emily.

They walked along eating cookies
and talking,
and soon they came to the river.

"I see our tent," said Emily,
"and my mother and father."

"And I hear my mother calling,"
said Little Bear.
"I have to go home for lunch.
Good-by, Emily."

"Good-by, Little Bear.

Come back and play with me."

"I will," said Little Bear.

Little Bear went skipping home.

He hugged Mother Bear and said,

"Do you know what I just did?"

"What did you just do, Little Bear?"

"I climbed to a treetop,
and I saw the wide world.
I climbed down again, and I saw
two squirrels, four little birds
and a little green worm.
Then I climbed all the way down,
and what do you think I saw?"

"What did you see?"

"I saw a little girl named Emily.
She was lost so I helped her
to get home.
And now I have a new friend.
Who do you think it is?"

"The little green worm,"
said Mother Bear.

Little Bear laughed.

"No," he said, "it is Emily.
Emily and I are friends."

Think and Respond

1 What does Little Bear see from the treetop?

2 What is the most important thing Little Bear does in the story? What else does he do?

3 Would you like to have a friend like Little Bear? Tell why or why not.

4 How can you tell that Little Bear and Emily will be friends?

5 What do you learn about Little Bear, his mother, and Emily from the story?

About the Author

Else Holmelund Minarik

Else Holmelund Minarik was four years old when she and her family left Denmark and moved to the United States. As a grown-up, she became a first-grade teacher. She began writing stories for children when she couldn't find good books for her first graders to read.

Else Holmelund Minarik wrote five books about Little Bear. The story you just read is from one of those books.

Meet the Illustrator

Maurice Sendak

Maurice Sendak grew up
in Brooklyn, in New York
City. He was the youngest of
three children. He remembers
his childhood well. He uses
his memories when he writes
and draws for children.
Maurice Sendak is one of
the most famous illustrators
of children's books.

Visit *The Learning Site!*
www.harcourtschool.com

Bears

Bears are playful.
Bears are round.
Grizzly bears
Are dressed in brown.

Bears like honey.
Bears like trees.
Bears are chased
By honeybees.

Bears like mountains.
Bears like streams.
Bears spend winters
In their dreams.

by Charles Ghigna
illustrated by Gabriel

Making Connections

Good Neighbor Skit

Little Bear is a very good neighbor. Work with a partner. Make up a skit that shows how to be a good neighbor.

Social Studies
CONNECTION

How Many in All?

In the story, Little Bear saw two squirrels, four birds, and one little green worm. First, draw all the animals. Next, write a number sentence. Then write the number of animals Little Bear saw in all.

2 + 4 + 1 =

Camping Fun

Emily and her family were camping by the river. Draw and write about Emily's camping trip.

Emily went fishing with her dad.

213

Alphabetize

Focus Skill

A B C D E F G H I J K L M N

Here are three animals Little Bear saw.

squirrel   **worm**   **bird**

Put these animal names in ABC order, or alphabetical order. To find out about these animals, you could look in a book that shows animals in alphabetical order.

- To find **bird,** would you look near the beginning or the end of the book?
- Would you find **worm** near the beginning or near the end?

Visit *The Learning Site!*
www.harcourtschool.com
See *Skills and Activities*

O P Q R S T U V W X Y Z

Test Prep
Alphabetize

1. Which word group is in alphabetical order?

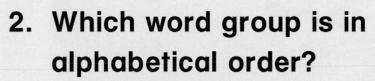

planet	comet	star
star	planet	comet
comet	star	planet
○	○	○

2. Which word group is in alphabetical order?

river	lake	lake
sea	sea	river
lake	river	sea
○	○	○

Tip

Read the words in the group. Look at the first letter of each word. Decide whether those letters are in ABC order.

▲ Busy Buzzy Bee

Word Power

Words to Remember

another

change

field

touch

twelve

wait

wild

216

We see lots of bees in our **field** .
They love the **wild** flowers there.
The bees **touch** the flowers and get
food from them.
Inside the hive, grubs **wait** for this food.
Soon the grubs will **change** into bees.
In about **twelve** days, there will be
another bunch of new bees.

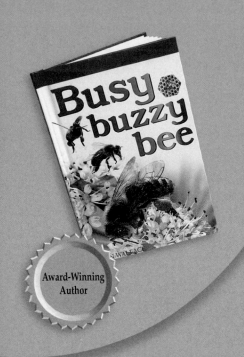

Nonfiction

In nonfiction, the author gives information about a subject.

Look for:

- Details about what worker bees do.

- Information about how bees grow.

- Information in the pictures.

Busy

Buzzy Bee

by Karen Wallace

z z z z z z z z z z z z z

Busy Bee has work to do.
She crawls out of her hive.

She spreads her wings.
Busy Bee is looking for a flower.

Busy Bee flies over a stream.

She flies past an oak tree and into a field.

The field is full of wild flowers.

Busy Bee lands on a flower.

Each flower holds sweet drops of nectar.
Bees make nectar into honey.
Nectar and honey are food for bees.

Busy Bee laps up the nectar with
her long, narrow tongue.
She will take it back to the hive.

Each flower holds grains of pollen.
Flower pollen is food for bees, too.

The pollen sticks to Busy Bee's
furry body.

She brings it to the hive on
her two back legs.

Busy Bee is a worker bee.

Inside the hive,
there are thousands like her.
All worker bees are female.

Busy Bee dances a dance.
She waggles her bottom.
She crawls in circles.
Her dance shows the other workers
the way to find the flower nectar.

Inside the hive,
the bees make cells.

Some are for the honey
the bees make from nectar.

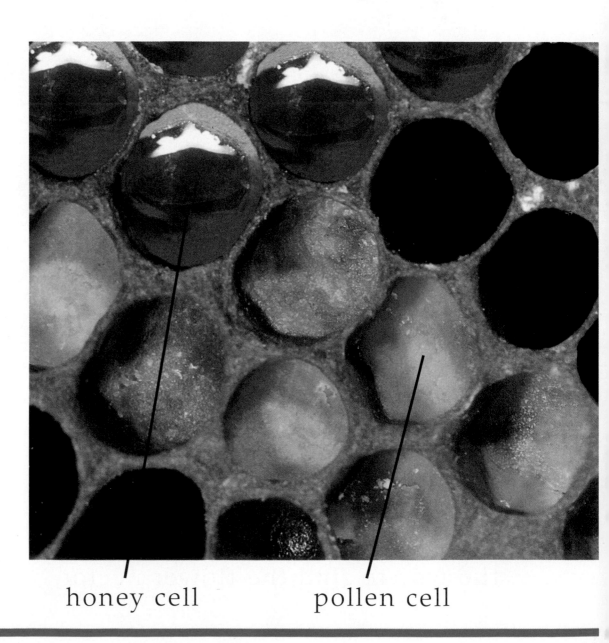

honey cell   pollen cell

Some are for the pollen
the bees have collected.

Some are for the eggs
that the queen bee lays.

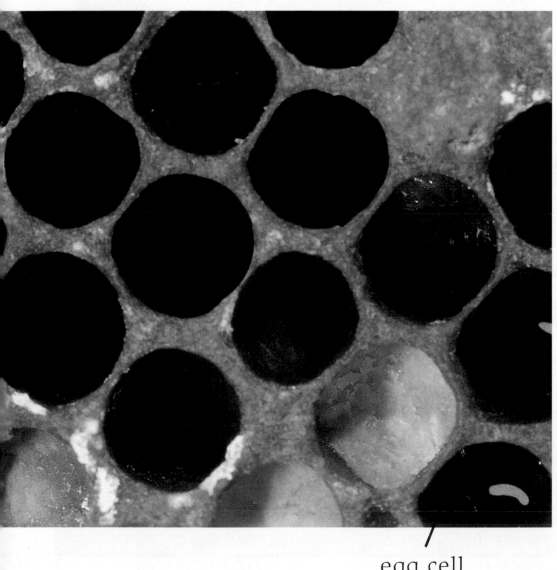

egg cell

Busy Bee has work to do.
First she feeds the drone bees.

All drones are male.
The drones mate with a queen bee.

Then Busy Bee feeds the queen bee.
The queen bee lays a thousand eggs
every day.
Inside their cells, the eggs hatch into
bee grubs.

Busy Bee and thousands like her
take some pollen mixed with honey.
They feed it to the hungry grubs.

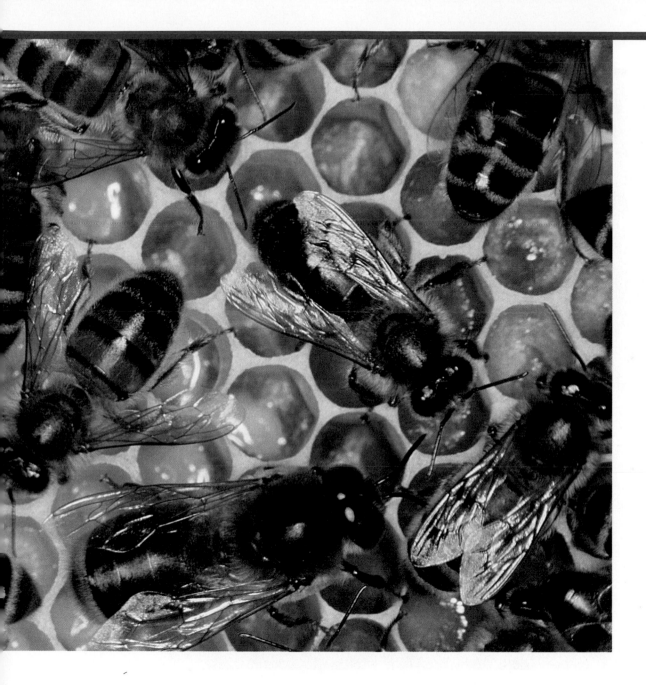

Busy Bee has work to do.
She feeds the bee grubs every day.
When the grubs are nine days old she
seals their cells with waxy covers.

Inside their cells,
the bee grubs change.
They grow legs and wings.
They grow long, narrow tongues.

In twelve days
they change from
grubs to bees.

They crawl out and wait
for their new wings to dry.

Busy Bee and thousands like her touch
the young bees with their feelers.

They make them welcome in the hive.
They feed them honey
from the cells.

Busy Bee has work to do.
The young bees are hungry.
Where can she find more
flower nectar?

Where can she find more
flower pollen?

Look!
Another bee is dancing!
She's found a garden
full of flowers.

She waggles her bottom.
She crawls in circles.
Her dance shows Busy Bee
how to find the garden.

241

Busy Bee and thousands like her fly
from the hive.

They find the garden full of flowers.
They drink the nectar.
They take the pollen.
Busy Bee has work to do.

Think and Respond

1 What keeps Busy Bee so busy?

2 The author begins and ends her story with the same sentence. What is it?

3 How are all the worker bees alike?

4 What happens to the eggs after the queen bee lays them?

5 Which fact did you think was the most interesting? Why?

Meet the Author

Karen Wallace

Karen Wallace grew up in a log
cabin in the woods of Quebec, in
Canada. She loved climbing trees
and playing by the river. Now
Karen Wallace lives in England
and writes books. She says, "The
way nature works is miraculous
and fascinating. Read about how
bees live together and then try
and imagine what it would be like
to be a bee. What would you see?
What would you think?"

Making Connections

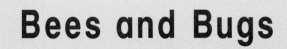

Bees and Bugs

Bees are insects. Find out about another kind of insect. How is it like a bee? How is it different? Share what you learn.

Science
CONNECTION

Animal Helpers

Honeybees make the honey we eat. What other good foods do we get from animals? Make a class chart.

Animals	Food Products

My Busy Day

Pretend you are Busy Bee. Draw and write about something you did today.

Today I welcomed the new bees.

247

Words with o-e

You know that <u>oa</u> and <u>ow</u> can stand for the long sound of <u>o</u>. Here are some words from "Busy Buzzy Bee" with that sound.

oak   **shows**   **grow**

Words with <u>o</u> followed by a consonant and <u>e</u> usually have the long sound of <u>o</u>, too.

drone

Write two words that rhyme with **drone.** You may want to use your Word Builder.

Test Prep
Long Vowel: /ō/ o-e

1. Which picture names have the long sound of <u>o</u>?

○   ○   ○

2. Which picture names have the long sound of <u>o</u>?

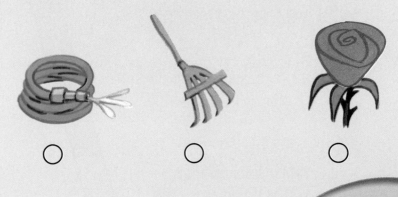

○   ○   ○

Tip

Say each picture name. Remember to listen for the vowel sound in each word.

Tips for Writing

Capital letters should be used only when they are needed.
Check your writing to be sure that you used capital
letters in the right places.

Capital letters should be used for:

- the first word
  of a sentence

  You are a good friend.

- the word <u>I</u>

  This is where I sit.

- people and pet names

  I like to play games with Jack.

- special places

  I live on Peach Street.

- days and months

  My birthday is the first
  Monday in June.

- holidays

  My grandma visits
  on Thanksgiving Day.

Every sentence needs an end mark. Check your writing to be sure that you used end marks correctly.

Follow these rules for end marks.

- Use a **period** at the end of a sentence that tells something.

This is *my* house.

- Use a **question mark** at the end of a sentence that asks something.

Where did the clown go?

- Use an **exclamation mark** at the end of a sentence that shows strong feeling.

That's the biggest balloon I've ever seen!

Sentences should tell what you really want others to know. Check to see if you need to add words to make your writing more interesting.

I found a dog.

I found a **big, brown** dog.

Friends came to my party.

Ten friends came to my **tea** party.

Models for Writing

You can look at these writing models when you need to write something special.

Friendly Letter

April 7, 2003

Dear Steven,
Today was field day at school. We had relay races. We played kickball and soccer. I won first place in the rope-climbing contest. We had a lot of fun!

Your friend,
Rodney

How-to Sentences

How to Draw a Boat

First, draw a rectangle. Next, draw a triangle. Then draw a line. Now you have a sailboat!

Words for Writing

People Words

baby

boy

doctor

girl

mail carrier

man

police officer

teacher

woman

Words for Writing

Holidays

Martin Luther
King, Jr. Day

Valentine's
Day

Presidents'
Day

Memorial Day

Independence Day

Labor Day

Columbus Day

Thanksgiving Day

Season and Weather Words

fall

winter

spring

summer

rain

snow

cold

hot

Glossary

What is a Glossary?

A glossary can help you read a word. You can look up the word and read it in a sentence. Some words have a picture to help you.

write Jane likes to **write** with a green pen.

a•bove   Write a 6 **above** the line.

above

a•gain   Can we read that book **again**?

al•most   The jar is **almost** full of marbles.

al•ways   Going to the ball game is **always** fun.

almost

an•y•thing   A goat will eat **anything**.

be•cause   I went to the doctor **because** I was sick.

257

cook

care   A vet takes **care** of animals.

change   A caterpillar can **change** into a butterfly.

cook   Dad and Peg **cook** dinner.

different

dif·fer·ent   My mittens are **different**.

Earth   We live on planet **Earth**.

258

field　The deer ran across the **field**.

front　Our school has a flag in **front** of it.

front

hel·lo　I say **hello** when someone calls.

high　The basket is too **high** to reach.

high

hold　**Hold** someone's hand when you cross the street.

know   Do you **know** what time it is?

love

lis•ten   I like to **listen** to the band.

love   I **love** my pet bunny.

most   Sara has the **most** books.

most

old   My **old** jacket does not fit.

on•ly   The baby **only** has one tooth.

o•ver   The tennis ball went **over** the net.

pret•ty   That is a **pretty** dress.

over

room   Our **room** has two beds.

room

say   What did you **say**?

sound   I can not hear a **sound**.

spe•cial   Today is my **special** day!

touch

touch   You can **touch** the soft fur.

town   We live in a **town** called Mill City.

twelve

twelve   The carton can hold **twelve** eggs.

wait   I must **wait** until it is my turn.

warm   Sunshine makes the day **warm**.

wa•ter   The bathtub is full of **water**.

wild   **Wild** pigs do not look like farm pigs.

water

write   Jane likes to **write** with a green pen.

years   Danny is three **years** old.

write

young   A **young** seal is called a pup.

Acknowledgments

For permission to reprint copyrighted material, grateful acknowledgment is made to the following sources:

Baronian Books: Illustration by Gabriel from "Bears" in *Animal Trunk: Silly Poems to Read Aloud* by Charles Ghigna. Illustration copyright © 1998 by Rainbow Grafics Intl-Baronian Books, Brussels.

Crown Publishers, Inc.: *Me on the Map* by Joan Sweeney, illustrated by Annette Cable. Text copyright © 1996 by Joan Sweeney; illustrations copyright © 1996 by Annette Cable.

Dorling Kindersley Ltd., London: *Busy Buzzy Bee* by Karen Wallace. Copyright © 1999 by Dorling Kindersley Limited, London.

Charles Ghigna: "Bears" from *Animal Trunk: Silly Poems to Read Aloud* by Charles Ghigna. Text copyright © 1999 by Charles Ghigna.

HarperCollins Publishers: "Little Bear and Emily" from *Little Bear's Friend* by Else Holmelund Minarik, illustrated by Maurice Sendak. Text copyright © 1960 by Else Holmelund Minarik; illustrations copyright © 1960 by Maurice Sendak.

Elizabeth M. Hauser: "Our Cat" from *Rhymes About Us* by Marchette Chute. Text copyright 1974 by E. P. Dutton.

National Wildlife Federation: "Our Homes Are Holes" from *Your Big Backyard* Magazine, July 1999. Text copyright 1999 by the National Wildlife Federation.

The Owl Group: "Visit the Robot Zoo" from *Chickadee* Magazine, Jan./Feb. 1998. Text © 1998 by Bayard Press.

Philomel Books, a division of Penguin Putnam Inc.: Illustration by Ed Young from *Cats Are Cats*, compiled by Nancy Larrick. Illustration copyright © 1988 by Ed Young.

Photo Credits

Key: (t) = top; (b) = bottom; (c) = center; (l) = left; (r) = right.
Page 29, Tom Sobolik / Black Star; 60, 61, Black Star; 66(l), Marty Loken/ Stone; 66(r), Roger Ressmeyer / Corbis; 67, VCG/FPG International; 68(l), Roger Ressmeyer / Corbis; 69, Marty Loken / Stone; 70, Bruno P. Zehnder / Peter Arnold, Inc.; 71(t), VCG/FPG International; 71(b), Wendy Watriss / Woodfin Camp & Associates; 72(t), Robert W. Weir / Corbis Stock Market; 72(b), Telegraph Colour Library / FPG International; 73(t), Martha Cooper / Peter Arnold, Inc.; 73(b), Robert Frerck / Woodfin Camp & Associates; 74, Fritz Prenzel / Peter Arnold, Inc.; 75, David Higgs / Corbis Stock Market; 76, Michael P. Gadomski / Photo Researchers, Inc.; 77(t), Hubertus Kanus / Photo Researchers, Inc.; 77(b), George Holton / Photo Researchers, Inc.; 78, Donald C. Johnson / Corbis Stock Market; 79(t), Corbis; 79(b), Nathan Benn / Corbis; 80, Adam Woolfitt / Woodfin Camp & Associates; 82, Frederica Georgia / Photo Researchers, Inc.; 83, Nebraska State Historical Society; 84(t), Fritz Polking / Peter Arnold, Inc.; 84(b), Nigel J. H. Smith / Earth Scenes; 85, Mike Yamashita / Woodfin Camp & Associates; 86(t), Viviane Moos / Corbis Stock Market; 86(b), Jeff Corwin / Photo Researchers, Inc.; 87, Chip Simons / FPG International; 88(tl), 88(tr), C. Karnow / Woodfin Camp & Associates; 88(b), LindsayHebberd / Woodfin Camp & Associates; 89(t), Douglas Waugh / Peter Arnold, Inc.; 89(b), Alan Schein / Corbis Stock Market; 90-91, Roger Ressmeyer / Corbis; 91, Rick Friedman / Black Star; 92(t), Animals Animals; 92(b), Thomas Kitchen / Tom Stack & Associates; 93(c), Michael P. Turco; 93(b), Kennan Ward; 94, 96(t), Marty Loken / Stone; 96(cl), Fritz Prenzel / Peter Arnold, Inc.; 96(cr), David Higgs / Corbis Stock Market; 96(bl), Nathan Benn / Corbis; 96(br), Donald C. Johnson / Corbis Stock Market; 119, Hector Amezquito / Black Star; 122, Michael P. Gadomski / Photo Researchers, Inc.; 144, 145, Black Star; 146(l)147, 148, 149, Robot Zoo; 154-177, Rick Friedman / Black Star; 178, Harcourt School Publishers; 179, 180(both), 183(all), Rick Friedman / Black Star; 208, courtesy, HarperCollins; 216(t), DK Publishing; 216(b), John Shaw / Bruce Coleman Collection; 217, 219(t), 218-219, DK Publishing; 220, D. Thompson / Earth Scenes; 221, Hans Reinhard / Bruce Coleman Collection; 222, Jena-Louis Le Moigne / NHPA; 223, DK Publishing; 224-225, John Shaw / Bruce Coleman Collection; 225, Stephen Dalton / NHPA; 226(both), DK Publishing; 227(t), Bruce Coleman Collection; 227(b), DK Publishing; 228-229, Bruce Coleman Collection; 230, Stephen Dalton / NHPA; 231, D. Thompson / Earth Scenes; 232-233, Jane Burton / Bruce Coleman Collection; 234, 235, 236-237, Stephen Dalton / NHPA; 238-239, Richard Coomber / Planet Earth Pictures; 240, Hans Reinhard / Bruce Coleman Collection; 242-243, DK Publishing; 244, 246-247, Hans Reinhard / Bruce Coleman Collection; 246(inset), Jena-Louis Le Moigne / NHPA; 256, Myrleen Ferguson / PhotoEdit; 257, Ken Kinzie / Harcourt School Publishers; 258, David Young-Wolff / PhotoEdit; 259, Dave Preston; 260, Rhoda Sidney /PhotoEdit; 261, Zefa Visual Media / Index Stock; 262, Amy Dunleavy; 263(b), Myrleen Ferguson / PhotoEdit.

Illustration Credits

Richard Cowdrey, Cover Art; Brenda York, 4-7; Holly Keller, 8-29; Ed Young, 30-31; Jo Lynn Alcorn, 32-33, 150; Liz Callen, 34-35, 97, 152-153; Annette Cable, 36-65; Christine Mau, 94; Jo Lynn Alcorn, 95; John Hovell, 95, 183, 246; Gerardo Suzán, 98-119; C. D. Hullinger, 120-121; Stacy Peterson, 122-123; Dagmar Fehlau, 124-145, 151; Steve Björkman, 151, 181; Linda Townshend, 184-185, 212, 214; Maurice Sendak, 186-209; Gabriel, 210-211; Clare Schaumann, 213, 249; Eldon Doty, 215; Ethan Long, 247.

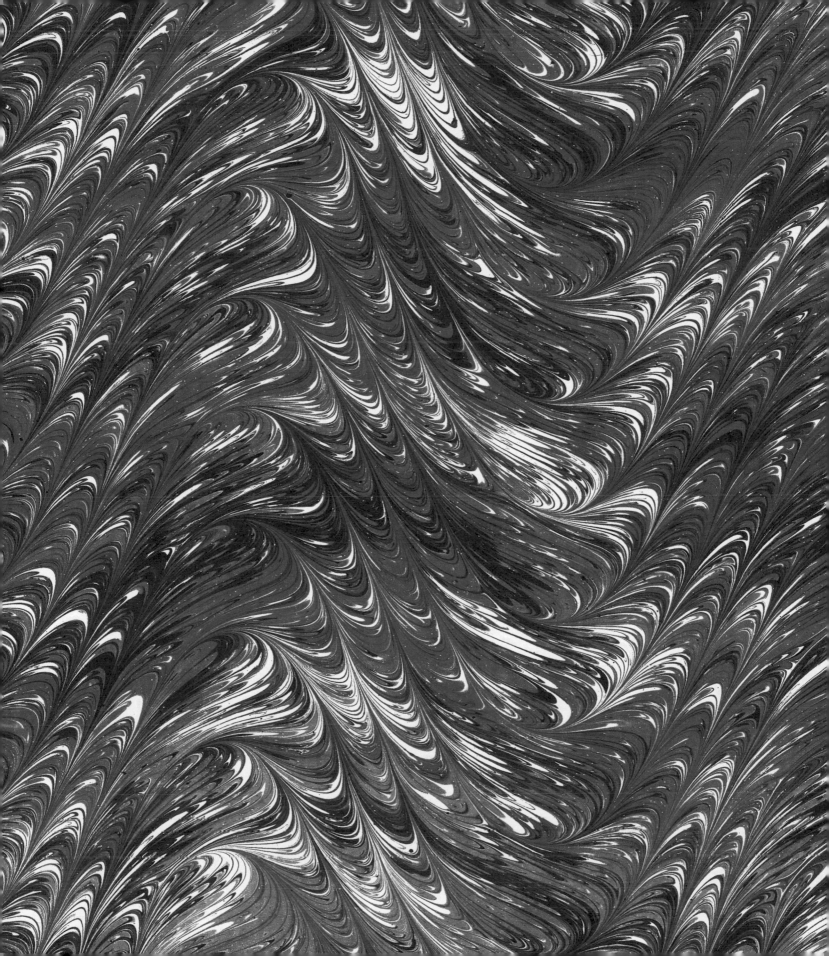

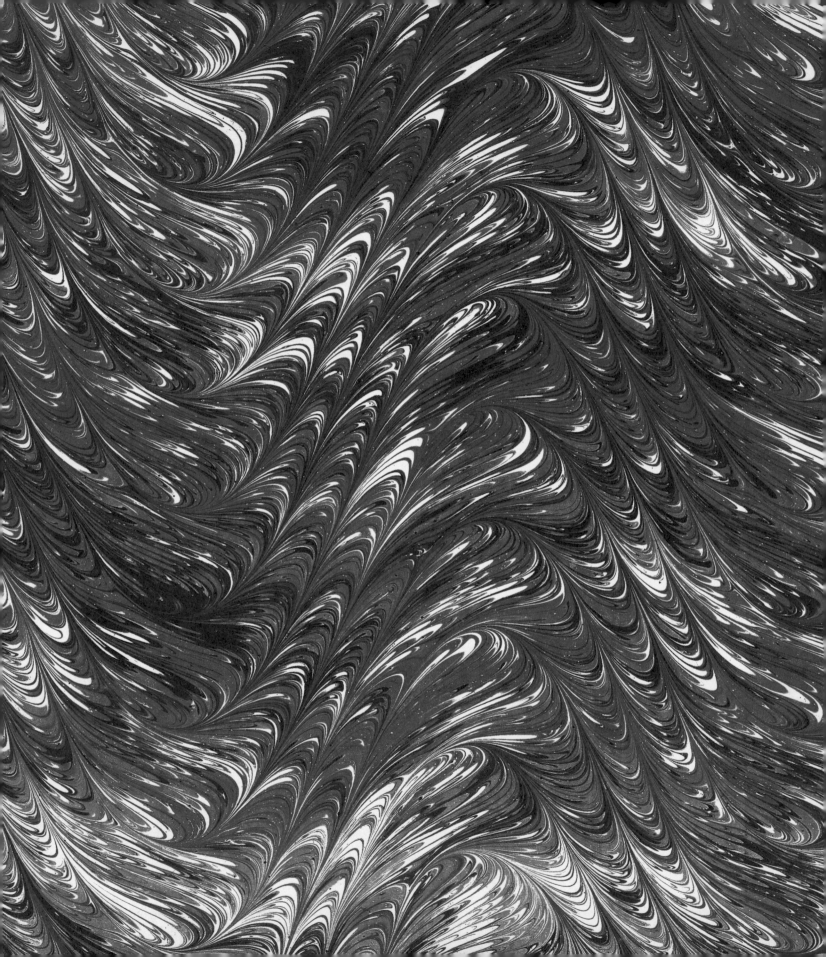